GEO

ACPL ITEM
DISCARDED

3/04

EDGE
BOOKS

DIRT BIKES

Motocross Racing

by Terri Sievert

Consultant:

Dirck J. Edge
Editor
MotorcycleDaily.com

Capstone
press

Mankato, Minnesota

Edge Books are published by Capstone Press
151 Good Counsel Drive, P.O. Box 669, Mankato, Minnesota 56002
www.capstonepress.com

Library of Congress Cataloging-in-Publication Data
Motocross Racing / by Terri Sievert.
    p. cm.—(Edge books. Dirt bikes)
    Summary: Discusses the history of motocross and supercross racing, some of the
competitive events, features of the dirt bikes used, safety equipment, and some of the
well-known personalities connected with this sport.
    Includes bibliographical references (p. 31) and index.
    ISBN 0-7368-2437-5 (hardcover)
    1. Supercross—History—Juvenile literature. 2. Trail bikes—History—Juvenile
literature. [1. Motocross. 2. Supercross. 3. Motorcycle racing. 4. Trail bikes.] I. Title.
II. Series.
GV1060.1455.S56 2004
796.7'56—dc22   2003013716

Editorial Credits
Angela Kaelberer, editor; Molly Nei, series designer; Jason Knudson, book designer;
    Jo Miller, photo researcher

Photo Credits
Anthony Scavo, 9, 21, 26
Corbis/AFP, cover; Mark Jenkinson, 20
Getty Images Inc./AFP/Koca Sulejmanovic, 5, 18; Robert Cianflone, 13, 14
Kinney Jones Photography, 6, 12
Photri-Microstock/John Powell, 17
SportsChrome-USA/Justin Silvey, 25
Steve Bruhn, 11, 23, 28, 29

Table of Contents

CHAPTER 1

Motocross Racing

Dust flies as a pack of motocross racers roars over a bumpy course. The riders lean right and left through the turns of the twisting course. Dirt sprays as a rider slides into a curve. The tires become caked with muck as the bike slogs through a mudhole.

Motocross racing is a tough sport. Riders race on rugged outdoor courses full of bumps and mudholes. The riders reach speeds as high as 75 miles (121 kilometers) per hour. Sharp turns test the riders' skills.

Learn about:
- History
- Early races
- Supercross

Motocross courses have bumps, curves, and steep jumps.

The name "supercross" comes from a motocross race held in California at the Los Angeles Coliseum in 1972. The race was called the "Super Bowl of Motocross." Later, people shortened this name to supercross.

Supercross events take place in large arenas.

Beginnings of Motocross

In 1924, motorcycle riders in England raced on a bumpy, rough outdoor course. People called the event a motorcycle scramble. Soon, other riders raced their bikes off-road. These racers began the sport of motocross.

The first major motocross race took place in Paris, France, in 1947. It was called Motocross des Nations. Teams from many countries raced against each other. That year, Great Britain's team won the race. Motocross des Nations is still held each year.

Growth of Motocross

In the late 1960s, motocross riders from Europe came to the United States to race. The skill of the European riders impressed U.S. fans. The sport gained popularity in the United States.

In the 1970s, people first held motocross races in stadiums and large arenas. These races are called supercross events. Later, arenacross became popular. Arenacross events take place in smaller arenas.

CHAPTER 2

Motocross Events

Racing groups set up motocross, supercross, and arenacross races. The American Motorcyclist Association (AMA) is in charge of many races in the United States. The Canadian Motorcycle Association (CMA) oversees races in Canada.

Riders compete in a series of races. Riders earn points in each race based on how they finish. The rider with the most points at the end of the season is the series champion.

Learn about:

- Tracks
- Scoring
- Freestyle

On January 4, 2003, Travis Pastrana raced in Anaheim, California.

Motocross Races

A motocross course is rough and hilly, with sharp turns and deep holes. The course has left and right turns. The turns have built-up corners called berms.

Jumps are scattered over the course. They can be as high as 20 feet (6 meters). Large jumps are at least 50 feet (15 meters) apart. Between some of the large jumps are smaller bumps called whoop-de-doos, whoops, or stutter bumps.

Events are divided into classes based on engine size. Engine size is measured in cubic centimeters (ccs). Most motocross and supercross cycles have 125cc or 250cc engines.

Each outdoor motocross event has two races called motos. In each moto, 20 racers earn points based on how they place. In AMA races, the first rider across the finish line gets 25 points. The second-place rider gets 22 points. The 20th finisher gets 1 point.

The scores from each moto are added for the rider's total points. The rider with the highest total points wins the event. When two riders' scores are tied, the rider who finished highest in the second moto is the winner.

Jumps are scattered over the motocross track.

Supercross Races

Most supercross races take place in large stadiums such as the Silverdome in Pontiac, Michigan. The courses are shorter than motocross courses. Most motocross courses are 1 to 2 miles (1.6 to 3.2 kilometers) long. Supercross courses are one-half mile (.8 kilometer) long. A supercross course has more jumps and tighter turns than a motocross course does.

Supercross racers first compete in short races called heats. Riders race around the track for eight laps. The top riders in each heat advance to the main event. The main event has 15 to 20 laps, depending on the class. The first rider to cross the finish line in the main event wins the race.

Supercross courses have tight turns.

Riders do triple jumps during races.

Arenacross

Arenacross races are often held in hockey or basketball arenas. The courses are about one-quarter mile (.4 kilometer) long.

Arenacross races include two motos, but they have a different scoring system than motocross and supercross events. The top finisher receives 20 points, while the second-place finisher receives 18 points. The rider who finishes in 18th place gets 1 point.

Tricks

Tracks have large bumps called jumps. A rider who goes over two jumps at once does a double. If a rider clears three jumps, the feat is called a triple.

Riders sometimes do tricks to celebrate during the last lap of a race. Riders may twist their bikes far to the side. They may also take their feet off the footpegs or their hands off the handlebars.

Some riders have given up racing and do only tricks. They may do a handstand on the bike or click their heels over the handlebars. These riders compete in freestyle contests.

CHAPTER 3

Power and Safety

Motocross and supercross bikes are built for off-road riding. They do not have a speedometer or turn signals. Instead, they have parts that help them handle the bumpy, rough courses.

Engines

In a motorcycle engine, a mixture of fuel and air is sprayed into a tube called a cylinder. The piston inside the cylinder moves up and down. After it moves up, a spark plug causes the fuel to explode. The explosion pushes the piston down and gives the bike power.

Learn about:
- Bike parts
- Shifting gears
- Safety

Dirt bikes are built for off-road riding.

Many dirt bikes have two-stroke engines. These engines produce power with two strokes of the piston. Two-stroke engines are both lightweight and powerful.

Riders use a twist grip and levers to control the bike's speed.

Some dirt bikes have four-stroke engines. These engines use four piston strokes to operate. Four-stroke engines are quieter and give off less pollution than two-stroke engines. But they are less powerful than two-stroke engines of the same size.

Changing Speed

The engine sends power to the bike's rear wheel through a drive chain. The drive chain slides around gears connected to the rear wheel.

Most dirt bikes have five gears that control the rear wheel's speed. To change speed, the rider must shift gears. To shift, the rider uses the clutch to release the drive chain. The rider controls the clutch with a lever on the left handlebar. The rider then uses the toes to push on the gearshift, which is under the left foot.

Each bike has a throttle on the right handlebar. The throttle controls the bike's speed by changing the amount of fuel and air sent to the engine. Riders twist the throttle to make the bike go faster. They let up on the throttle to slow down the bike.

Dirt bikes have two braking systems.

Exhaust and Suspension Systems

Engines release waste from burned fuel through exhaust pipes. The pipes on two-stroke engines have a bulge called an expansion chamber. The chamber uses the pressure from the released exhaust to pump more air and gas into the cylinders. This action gives the engine extra power.

A dirt bike's suspension system makes a ride on a rough track smoother. The front fork connects the front wheel to the frame. The shock absorbers inside the front fork cushion the front tire from bumps. Another shock absorber cushions bumps that hit the back tire.

Tires and Brakes

Motocross racing bikes have knobby tires with deep grooves. These treads grip dirt and mud better than smooth tires do. The front tire is narrower and larger in diameter than the rear tire. This feature gives the rider good control.

The front and rear tires have separate braking systems. Riders control the front brake with a lever on the right handlebar. Riders press a lever with the right foot to slow down the rear tire.

Racing bikes have knobby tires.

Safety Gear

Helmets help protect riders from head injuries. The outer helmet is made of hard, lightweight material such as polycarbonate or carbon fiber. Stiff foam inside the helmet holds the rider's head still and protects it from bumps.

Riders' clothing is designed to both protect the rider's body and be comfortable. Riders wear long-sleeved shirts made of polyester or another lightweight material that allows the skin to breathe. Pants are made of tough, lightweight materials such as nylon and neoprene.

Riders wear hard plastic body armor to protect against injuries. The body armor covers the chest, shoulders, thighs, knees, and elbows.

Gloves protect the riders' hands. They are made of soft material with hard plastic or padding sewn into them.

Boots with thick soles cover the rider's feet and ankles. The tall boots have plastic shin plates to help protect riders' lower legs. Metal toe caps protect riders' toes.

Body armor protects a rider's chest from injury.

CHAPTER 4

Motocross Stars

Ricky Carmichael is not afraid of speed. He whips around tight corners at speeds up to 60 miles (97 kilometers) per hour. His skills have set racing records and earned him many national motocross and supercross titles.

Carmichael was born in 1979 in Florida. He started racing at age 5 and won nine amateur national titles by age 15. He turned pro at 16 and won seven AMA Motocross Series titles between 1997 and 2003.

Learn about:
- Ricky Carmichael
- Jeremy McGrath
- Rising stars

Ricky Carmichael has won more pro races than any other rider.

Jeremy McGrath won seven Supercross Series titles during his pro career.

Carmichael won his first AMA 250cc Supercross Series title in 2001 and won again in 2002. He then set a motocross record by winning 24 straight motos to take the 2002 AMA 250cc Motocross Series title.

In 2003, Carmichael again was the AMA Supercross and Motocross Series champion. That year, he won his 99th pro race and set an AMA record for the number of pro career wins.

King of Supercross

Jeremy McGrath was born in San Francisco, California, in 1971. He began racing at age 14 and turned pro in 1989. He won his first AMA Supercross Series championship in 1993.

Fans call McGrath the "King of Supercross." He won 74 supercross races and seven AMA Supercross Series titles during his career. He retired from racing after the 2002 season.

Jeremy McGrath invented one of the first freestyle tricks, the nac-nac. In midair, McGrath swung one leg behind him and over to the other side. He looked like a rider getting off a horse.

New Stars

In 1985, 3-year-old Chad Reed began riding dirt bikes near his home in Australia. Reed turned pro at 16 and won the Australian Supercross Championship in 2000. In 2001, he finished second in the 250cc class of the World Grand Prix Motocross Series. Reed then moved to California to race. He won the AMA Eastern Region 125cc Supercross title in 2002.

In 2003, Chad Reed finished just seven points behind AMA 250cc Supercross champion Ricky Carmichael.

At 16, James Stewart Jr. was named 2002 AMA Rookie of the Year.

James Stewart Jr. of Haines City, Florida, is another new motocross star. He began racing at age 4 and turned pro in 2002 at age 16. That year, Stewart won the AMA 125cc Motocross title and was named the AMA Rookie of the Year. He was the youngest racer ever to win a national motocross title.

Each year, motocross racers move up from the amateur to the professional ranks. These new stars will continue to take the sport to a higher level.

Glossary

berm (BURM)—a banked turn or corner on a motocross course

clutch (KLUHCH)—a lever on the handlebar that allows a motocross rider to shift gears

cylinder (SIL-uhn-dur)—a hollow tube inside an engine where fuel is burned to create power

neoprene (NEE-uh-preen)—a strong, waterproof material sometimes used to make motocross clothing

piston (PIS-tuhn)—a part inside an engine cylinder that moves up and down as fuel burns

polycarbonate (pol-ee-CAR-buh-nayt)—a strong plastic material often used to make motocross helmets

throttle (THROT-uhl)—a twist grip that controls the amount of fuel and air that flows into an engine

Read More

Freeman, Gary. *Motocross.* Radical Sports. Chicago: Heinemann Library, 2003.

Herran, Joe, and Ron Thomas. *Motocross.* Action Sports. Philadelphia: Chelsea House, 2004.

Parr, Danny. *Dirt Bikes.* Wild Rides! Mankato, Minn.: Capstone Press, 2002.

Useful Addresses

American Motorcyclist Association
13515 Yarmouth Drive
Pickerington, OH 43147-8273

Canadian Motorcycle Association
P.O. Box 448
Hamilton, ON L8L 1J4
Canada

Internet Sites

FactHound offers a safe, fun way to find Internet sites related to this book. All of the sites on FactHound have been researched by our staff.

Here's how:

1. Visit *www.facthound.com*
2. Type in this special code **0736824375** for age-appropriate sites. Or enter a search word related to this book for a more general search.
3. Click on the **Fetch It** button.

FactHound will fetch the best sites for you!

Index